HOW TO IMPROVE YOUR QUILTING STITCH

By Ami Simms

Illustrations by
Jean Pajot Smith

MALLERY PRESS
Flint, Michigan

DEDICATION

For Ida who got me hooked on quilts in the first place, Steve who gently encourages my "addiction," Jennie who will have to learn to quilt in self defense, Caron who dangled the first carrot, and Mom who leads the cheering section.

Third Edition.
HOW TO IMPROVE YOUR QUILTING STITCH. Copyright © 1987 by Ami Simms. Printed and bound in the United States of America. ALL RIGHTS RESERVED. No part of this book may be reproduced or transmitted in any form, or by any means, electronic or mechanical, including but not limited to photocopying, recording, or by any informational storage or retrieval system without written permission from the publisher, except by a reviewer who may quote brief passages in a review.

Published by Mallery Press
4206 Sheraton Drive
Flint, Michigan 48532-3557 USA
Telephone: 1-800-A-STITCH or (810) 733-8743

Library of Congress Cataloging in Publication Data

Simms, Ami, 1954–
   How to improve your quilting stitch.

   1. Quilting.   I. Smith, Jean Pajot.   II. Title
TT835.S54   1987   746.9'7   87-12575

ISBN 0-943079-00-4

CONTENTS

INTRODUCTION

The first quilting stitch I ever took was at a quilting bee in an Old Order Amish home. I had just met the women seated around the frame when they asked me if I'd like to sew with them. I picked up a needle, threaded it, and promptly jammed it through the quilt and into my finger.

With great difficulty, I managed to work the needle back up through the layers of the quilt to complete my first enormous stitch. Having made my "toe-hooker" I glanced around the frame only to see the other women guiding their needles in and out of the fabric as if it required absolutely no effort at all.

My second stitch wasn't much better. In fact, it was even longer. And, in order to make my third stitch, I seem to remember asking the woman sitting next to me to move her chair just a little because I was running out of room!

Since that summer afternoon more than a decade ago I'm pleased to say I've made some improvement. I no longer measure my quilting stitches in "inches per stitch," but rather, in "stitches per inch," and I've learned that there are certain variables that can be manipulated to help ensure smaller, more even stitches.

This book is a detailed examination of those variables. Some you may already be familiar with, some you may never have thought of, and some you may feel are not worth the compromises.

While you may decide not to turn each variable to your advantage in every quilt, understanding how they can contribute to smaller stitches can help you become a better quiltmaker.

Have fun and enjoy!

CHAPTER I
THE QUILT
Fabric

Modern innovative quiltmakers are using everything from filmy organza to corduroy and fake fur — sometimes all in the same quilt. They are making wonderful design statements in color and texture, and challenging us to stretch our imaginations. Quiltmakers are no longer limited to traditional designs or traditional fabrics. Almost anything goes.

Whether you're a trend-setter or a traditionalist, all quilts must eventually be quilted, and the fabrics you choose will make a difference in the quality of stitch you are able to make. Obviously, heavier fabrics are harder to stitch than lighter ones. Lightweight shirting beats broadcloth any day.

Leather and lamé aside, most quilters simply debate over using a cotton/polyester blend or 100% cotton fabric in their quilts. The best choice for small even stitches is a good quality 100% cotton fabric. It is easier to pierce with a needle, and offers less resistance as the needle is guided in and out of each stitch.

To test this point, stretch pieces of cotton and cotton/polyester fabric on a hoop. Jab a needle straight down several times into each. The polyester blend will offer more resistance.

The best cotton to work with is one which has a high opacity or thread density. This does not always mean a higher thread count, however, a fact patiently explained to me by Jeffrey Gutcheon. High thread count only refers to the number of threads per inch, and does not necessarily take into consideration the thickness of each thread. Many thin or weak threads per inch may not be as good as fewer, thicker or stronger ones.

When purchasing fabric, hold it up to the light. Generally, the ones through which the least amount of light can be seen are of the best quality.

Good quality 100% cotton fabric used as a backing will make the quilt easier to needle as well. Even though many quilters prefer to use 100% cotton bed sheets as backings for large quilts because they do not require seaming, this kind of cloth is not as pliable as 100% cotton fabric cut from the bolt, and thus is more difficult to quilt through.

Keep in mind, however, that cotton fabric is more expensive, will fade more rapidly with washing and exposure to sunlight, and gives the quilt a flatter appearance than does a cotton/polyester blend fabric.

Batting

Batting makes a difference, too. The thinner the batting, the easier it is to manipulate the needle, and the smaller the stitch.

For many years I used a medium-weight bonded polyester batting. I was pleased with the way my quilts looked but didn't pay too much attention to the length of my stitches. I figured that was just the best I would ever be able to do.

When I was no longer able to purchase the batting locally, I reluctantly changed to a different brand. It, too, was a bonded polyester batt, but it was about half the thickness. I was amazed at the difference. It was easier to quilt because of the reduced bulk, and I was able to get smaller stitches with very little effort.

There is a great variety of good batting available on the market. At no time have we "needle pushers" had a greater selection. Sample as many different products as you can before deciding on the right batting for a particular project. Collect leftover scraps of batting from your past projects, borrow pieces from other quilters, mail-order from quilt shops faraway, or write directly to the batting manufacturers to see what your options are. (See APPENDIX A for a list of the major batting manufacturers and their addresses.)

Perform two tests on each sample. First, quilt on each one. Check for bulkiness and ease of quilting.

Second, make a potholder-sized-mini-whole cloth quilt on the sewing machine. Use the same fabric you selected for the quilt top you are preparing to quilt, or black fabric all from the same bolt. Machine quilt it just to hold the three layers together, and bind it off.

Machine wash and dry each mini-quilt twice, making sure the water temperature, agitation time and dryer setting are the same for each sample, if they are not all tested at the same time. This is no way to treat a quilt, but it should give you a good idea of how the batting will hold up after several years of use and gentle laundering.

Look for bearding (batting fibers that are sticking out of the fabric), pilling (little balls or globs of batting appearing on the quilt's surface) shifting or bunching, and overall loft. On the basis of these two tests, decide which batting is acceptable and which is not.

CHAPTER II
THE QUILTING STRATEGY

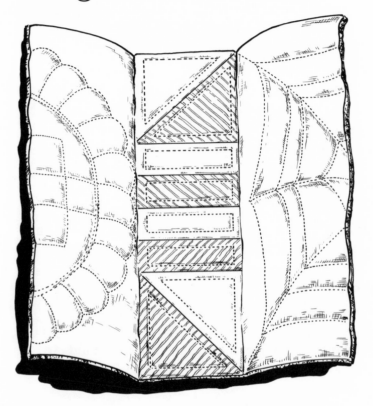

The quilting motifs you choose and the method in which you quilt them can have an effect on the ease with which you make your stitches and thus their size. Will you quilt an elaborate design with intricate curves, simply outline each piece in the block a quarter inch from the seam, or combine the two? There are several points to consider.

Direction

Whatever the quilting pattern, try to quilt in the most comfortable way possible. If working in a hoop or in your lap, rotate the quilting surface so that you are sewing in the direction that is easiest for you. For most right-handed quilters, this means sewing from right to left, from top to bottom, or diagonally from the upper right-hand corner down towards the lower left-hand corner. For left-handed quilters the reverse is true.

If you work on a frame you must learn to rotate your body in relation to the quilting surface, and put up with an occasional awkward quilting position. Try using a swivel chair or moving slightly to one side of the quilting area to get a better angle.

Thankfully, most quilting motifs, even ones that appear complicated, can be quilted in your favorite direction if you take a few seconds to locate the best places to start and stop each thread.

"Traveling," or sliding the needle just under the quilt top to get from one part of the quilting design to the other is another strategy to consider. Just be sure that the traveling thread never shows on top or back, and that the distance you travel is not too great. A good rule of thumb is to only travel one needle's length away.

Proximity To Seams

Avoid quilting through seam allowances whenever possible. Extra layers of fabric increase the resistance on your needle and make it extremely difficult to form the stitches. Quilting in the ditch, immediately to one side of the seam allowance, is only slightly less difficult. While you can get away with a lot less quilting, the extra layers of fabric are still working against you. Worse yet, the stitches are almost hidden. What's the point of hand quilting if no one can admire your efforts?

Quilting one quarter inch from the seamline, a popular quilting strategy, is easier yet, especially on the side of the seam farthest from the seam allowance.

Quilting away from the influence of seam allowances is the easiest. The wide, open spaces of large pieces are especially pliable. The quilt gives more and can easily bend on and off the needle with each stitch. Keep in mind, however, that the first line of stitching must compress and draw all three layers of the quilt together. Once this has been accomplished you will have an easier time of it.

Grainline

Grainline can also make a difference in the way quilting stitches turn out. Forming stitches on the straight of the goods, WITH the grainline, (parallel to the selvage edge) is more difficult than quilting CROSS GRAIN (perpendicular to the selvage edge). More pressure is required to form each stitch. You may even notice that the stitches appear to be "swallowed" by the fabric when sewing with the grain. This is especially apparent when working with cotton blends, another reason to stick with 100% cotton fabrics.

Stitching cross grain is easier because the fabric has slightly more give. Quilting on the bias where the fabric stretches the most, is the easiest of all. The more the fabric is able to bend, the easier it is to needle and make smaller stitches. (To learn how to find grainline, please refer to Appendix B.)

CHAPTER III
THE TOOLS
Marking

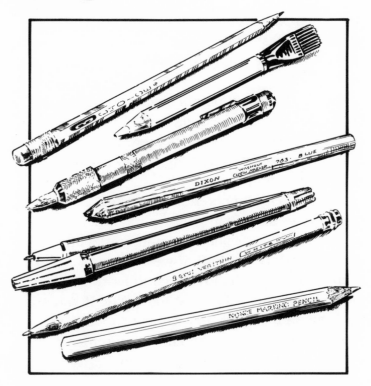

Whether you mark your quilt top with curves or straight lines, elaborate innovative designs or the old standbys, use a marking tool that does the job. It should be easy to use, give a clear, easily visible line, and completely disappear after it has served its purpose.

There are many marking tools to choose from. Consider each alternative carefully and BE SURE TO TEST EACH ONE THOROUGHLY BEFORE YOU MAKE UP YOUR MIND.

For years pencils have been the tool of choice. Pencil marks show up on all light colored fabrics and on some darks as well. A hard lead (higher number) is preferable to a soft lead. The line is harder to see, but will wash out with more success. A dashed line, or a series of dots is better than a continuous line for the same reason.

Keep the pencil point consistently sharp and take care to wash the quilt thoroughly when it is completed. Nothing detracts more from beautifully executed quilting stitches than a leftover pencil line!

Chalk is also a perennial favorite. Dressmaker's chalk in white, pink, blue, and yellow comes in pencil form and marks on almost every color cloth. It wears down fast, so keep a sharpener handy. In contrast to graphite (pencil), it comes off almost too easily. If you are working on a project that will take a while to complete and will be handled often, remarking the quilting lines several times may be necessary.

Soapstone pencils make a white line that is easy to see on dark colored cloth, but is virtually invisible on lighter colors. The line will stay longer than chalk, but requires considerably more downward force to make. Again, a pencil sharpener will be useful.

Water soluble pencils, a more recent innovation, come in white, rose, red, blue, and green and make a clear, visible line on all colors. The lines have more staying power than chalk

and are easily removed. Simply dab them off
with cool water. Some brands may require more
coaxing with a wet cloth to disappear than
others. Some work better on some fabrics than
on others. Keep a sharpener nearby; and be
prepared to redraw quilting lines periodically, if
the project will be handled often.

Water soluble markers have been around for
at least fifteen years. These "felt-tip" type
markers make a clear light blue, purple or pink
line on light and medium hues. Another tool is
recommended for use on darker colors. The
beauty of these markers (and the water soluble
pencils mentioned above, for that matter) is that
they are great for sloppy quilters who make lots
of mistakes when they mark. Unwanted lines can
be "erased" with cold water and redrawn after
the fabric has dried.

Be sure to read the directions on the back of
the package carefully. Some laundry detergents
set the lines and turn them brown, permanently.
To avoid problems, don't blot the markings away
with a damp cloth or mist them off with a spray
bottle. Instead, dunk your finished project in a
clean and well rinsed bathtub filled with cool
water until it is completely saturated. This
should remove any lingering marks. If you feel
you must wash the quilt, drain the water and
refill the tub with clean water before adding a
mild soap.

Pencils used for marking on blueprints are
now in vogue with many quilters. They come in

assorted colors and can be purchased at office supply stores, quilt shops, or blueprint supply houses. White and silver work very well on dark colored fabrics and wash out fairly easily.

White, wax based pencils are also a popular tool for marking quilts. They leave a mark that is not easily brushed off during the quilting process; however, repeated washings may be required to totally remove the marks.

Whatever tool you decide on, take the time to TEST IT THOROUGHLY BEFORE YOU USE IT. TEST IT ON EVERY PIECE OF FABRIC YOU INTEND TO USE IT ON. Test it for visibility. Does it make a line that you can see well enough to follow? Test for "iron-ability." Will a hot iron set the marks? Test for washability. Will gentle hand laundering remove ALL the marks?

Stretching and Basting

Once the quilt top is marked, take care to stretch and baste the three layers (top, batting and back) together carefully. It is best to do this on a traditional frame of "one by twos" and C-clamps. "One by twos" are long, narrow boards that actually only measure 3/4 x 1 3/4 inches. They should run at least the length of your quilt plus 4 inches to accommodate the C-clamps. They are called 1 x 2s by the lumber industry as those are the dimensions of the wood before it is run through the saw.

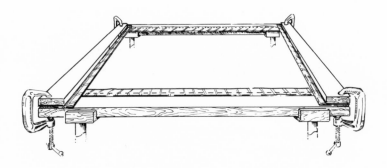

A simple frame of 1 x 2s and C-clamps.

Staple or nail strips of fabric to the boards with about a 2 inch overhang so that the three layers of the quilt can be pinned to the fabric with ease.

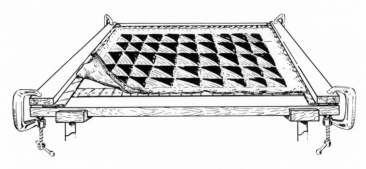

The quilt is pinned to the frame.

Use basting thread or small non-rusting brass safety pins to hold the layers together until they are quilted. Proper stretching and close basting will ensure that your quilt top will be uniformly matched with the other two layers, and will handle as one piece of cloth, not three individual pieces, freeing you to concentrate more fully on your quilting stitches.

Frames, Hoops, or Laps

When you begin to quilt, will you use a frame, a hoop or your lap? The method you choose may improve your quilting stitch.

My personal favorite is a simple frame of "one by twos." I use the same frame to quilt as I do to stretch. I simply replace two of the long boards that I used in stretching, with two smaller ones (about 24 inches long) and roll the basted quilt to fit.

Working on a frame is comfortable for me because that's how I learned to quilt. I find I am able to make smaller stitches because the quilt is uniformly stretched and taut, and I don't have to be a contortionist trying to hold the quilt AND sew at the same time. My concentration is focused on my quilting and I don't have to worry about hanging on to the quilt.

An extra bonus is that the quilt stays cleaner because it never touches the floor, and I stay cooler because the quilt is not draped over my lap. To take a break all I need do is stop quilting, stand up, and walk away. There is nothing to "put away." The only disadvantage is the space it takes up.

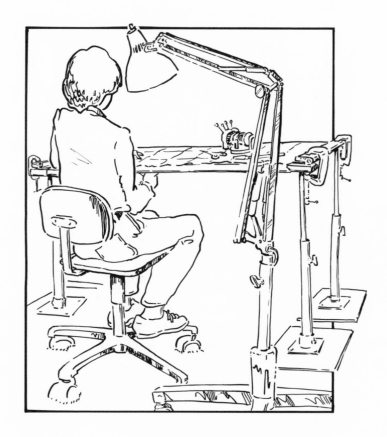

The author at the frame.

Quilting in a hoop is the next best thing to quilting on a frame, but only if the hoop is supported by a lap or floor pedestal.

Hoop supported by a pedestal.

For me, hand held hoops come in third, and lap quilting comes in a poor fourth. Without the tension on the quilt from either a frame or a hoop I find it very hard to make small stitches.

Needles

It **is** true. The shorter the needle, the smaller the stitch, up to a point. My first quilts were quilted with an embroidery needle! I figured a needle was a needle was a needle.

It took a lot of convincing to get me to give up that old friend and try a shorter "between." I tried a number seven and noticed an improvement immediately. The shorter, thinner needle was easier to maneuver in and out of the quilt, giving me better control and smaller stitches.

With still more prodding from my quilting friends I moved up to a nine. Again the smaller needle helped to improve my stitches.

Recently I figured that if a nine was good, then a twelve must be better. Unfortunately, smaller needles only improved my quilting stitches up to a point. I found the disadvantages of threading the smaller needle far outweighed the slightly smaller stitches I was able to make with it. For me, it was not worth the effort. So I compromised and switched to a #10.

There are many brands of needles on the market these days. Again, I urge you to experiment with as many different brands and sizes as you can to see which ones you like. Some bend easily, others have a tendency to break off at the tip.

Look for a short needle that is easy to thread, and able to withstand the force of your quilting stitch. It should be sturdy, sharp and straight.

Avoid bent needles. They are unpredictable. Having to guess where the needle will exit the quilt takes your mind off the task at hand. Besides, it can be painful.

Change needles often. If you use the same

needle all the time it will eventually become dull.
When it is too dull to use, or when it bends or
breaks, and you are forced to use a new one, you
may have some trouble adjusting to the sharper
needle. Pushing on a dull needle requires more
force than pushing a sharp one.

Thimbles

Don't forget the importance of a good
thimble. Look for thimbles that have deep
indentations on the top to really grab the eye of
the needle allowing you to put as much pressure
as possible to bring the point of the needle up
through the layers of fabric.

The best metal thimbles I have seen come
from Spain and Germany. Also, if you can find
them, many antique silver and brass thimbles
have adequate "dimples." I have also seen some
very good polystyrene (plastic) thimbles from
England and Austria.

Some enterprising quilting suppliers are soldering metal rings around the tops of thimbles to make up for the lack of good indentations. Recently some manufacturers have come out with a metal thimble with a raised edge. They're better than the "flat-tops" without the ring, but are still very awkward, allowing the top of the needle to slop from one side of the thimble to the other.

Many tailor's thimbles (those without a top) have good indentations, but they are difficult to quilt with. The side of the thimble is too curved to anchor the eye of the needle in the indentations. Should it slip out, it could jab one of the fingers on either side. I prefer to push from the top of the thimble, where I am able to exert more force.

Leather thimbles grab the eye of the needle nicely, and will protect your fingers if only single stitches are taken. If you elect to "rocker quilt" and take as many as five or six small tight stitches on your needle before pulling the thread through, I doubt that the leather thimble will stand up to the pressure of the needle for long.

Many quilters also use a thimble on the hand that works the underside of the quilt. I discourage the practice because it keeps the quilter from feeling the presence of the needle as it comes down through the quilt. If you want to make small stitches, it is extremely important to anticipate the needle with a good sense of touch.

A thimble, even a thin leather one, obscures this. The same goes for metal plates, spoons, layers of nail polish, adhesive tape, bandages, masking tape, dried glue and other gadgets currently in vogue. With practice and concentration you CAN learn NOT to jam the needle into your finger with every stitch!

CHAPTER IV
THE QUILTING ENVIRONMENT
Light

Good, bright light is essential if small stitches are the goal. Quilting in a well-lighted room is not enough. A gooseneck, architect's, or "quilter's lamp" that will focus bright light on the quilting surface is a must. Use at least a 75 watt bulb and direct the lamp so that the light will reflect off the point of the needle as it comes up through the top of the quilt.

Position the light on your left (on your right if you are left-handed) to let the light shine across your workspace and onto the needle. Clamp-on lamps can be fastened directly to the quilting frame or onto a nearby piece of furniture. If there is ample floor space, a simple stand can be built to accommodate a light source. (I took the swivel legs off a dilapidated chair and mounted an architect's lamp to it using a length of electrical conduit and a thumb screw.)

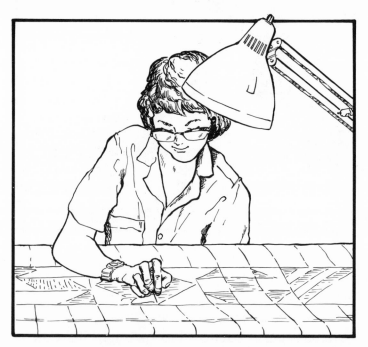

Proper light positioning.

Adjust the light each time you change directions or move several inches one way or the other. It takes only a few seconds and can make a big difference. Remember, the only clue to the length of the top stitch before pulling the thread through is the amount of needle that is showing on the top of the quilt. If you can't see the light shining off the needle, you might just as well quilt in the dark.

The Weather

It may sound silly, but even the weather can affect the size of your quilting stitch. In warm or humid weather (or in an overheated room) your hands will perspire. The moisture can oxidize the needle (turn it black) and make it stick as it goes in and out of the fabric. You try to compensate, push harder, and find that the needle went too far — into your finger! Unpredictable needles make small stitches almost impossible.

CHAPTER V
THE QUILTER

Experience

Experience plays a part, too. The more you quilt, the better you will get, if you make even a small effort. You'll probably see improvement as you work on a single quilt.

Think, for example, of the first stitches you put in each day. They're usually the worst. Until your fingers "warm up" stitching can feel awkward and look funny, too. As you get used to moving the needle around, your stitches improve. If you feel your first stitches of the day mar the quilt, warm up on something else, or quilt a few inches with an UNthreaded needle until you get the feel back.

Returning to a quilt after several days (weeks, months?!) off can make stitching seem really foreign. If you can, try to quilt a little every day, even if it's just a few stitches.

Each time you finish a quilt, try and find the first stitches you put in. How do they stack up to the last ones you sewed? You've probably improved as you worked through the quilt.

Whether you quilt in front of the "idiot box" (TV) or think profound thoughts while you push your needle, take some time to think about what you're doing and make every stitch count.

Your Mental Outlook

Your emotional frame of mind has some part to play in the quality of your stitches as well. The exhilaration of success ("Wow! Look at those great little stitches these fingers of mine just made!") spurs you on to even greater successes. Similarly, frustration and fear of failure can inhibit the quilter with even the best potential.

Relax and enjoy the learning process. Quilting is supposed to be challenging, but fun. World peace doesn't rest on the size of your quilt stitches. Concentrate and let your work improve, while you enjoy the process.

If frustration is making the project seem like a chore, move onto something else. Unless you are making a commissioned work that needs to be finished by a certain date, take some time off.

CHAPTER VI
THE QUILTING STITCH

The "Simple" Running Stitch

The quilting stitch always sounds too good to be true. In fact, it sounds like the same stitch your mother taught you when you first learned how to sew. The needle goes in and out of the layers of cloth, making stitches on the top and bottom. You push the needle as you coax the fabric onto it. When you don't have any more room on the needle, you hold onto the cloth and pull the thread through. Then you do it again. When you first heard that quilting is nothing but a running stitch, you thought it would be a snap, right?

Making a small running stitch while holding the fabric and being able to see both your hands is one thing. Executing a respectable quilting stitch with one hand hiding under the quilt is quite another. Quilting and hand piecing are two different skills.

The Real World

There are three ways to make a quilting stitch. All are acceptable if you can execute them well. In order of ascending efficiency they are:

stab stitching, single stitching, and rocker quilting.

Stab Stitching

When stab stitching, the needle is inserted from the top of the quilt with one hand, travels down through the batting and back, and is retrieved under the quilt with the other hand. To complete the stitch, the needle is then reinserted from beneath the quilt, travels up through the back and batting and emerges again on the top of the quilt. One stitch is taken at a time.

For most, it is a slow and inaccurate way to go. Stitches on the top of the quilt can be made to follow a specific quilting line and can look very nice, but stitches on the back tend to be long and lopsided. This is because the quilter aims for a point on the quilt top where the needle will exit and has to guess where the needle enters the back of the quilt.

There are times, however, when nothing but a stab stitch will get you through a difficult area. In applique, for instance, when there are many thicknesses of fabric to be quilted through (the joining of many seams that can't be trimmed away) and the quilt will not bend on and off a needle, then a stab stitch can be a lifesaver.

Single Stitching

Single stitching is much more accurate than stab stitching. It is worked from the top of the quilt with two fingers and the thumb of the top hand, and one finger on the bottom hand working from beneath the quilt.

NOTE: All instructions refer to top and bottom hands. If you are right-handed, your right hand is the top hand. If you are left-handed, the reverse is true. All illustrations in the text picture a right-handed quilter. Left-handed quilters are invited to refer to Appendix D.

This kind of quilting involves pressure on the top (eye) of the needle at two different times and in two different directions. It necessitates both a light touch and alternately, considerable force. Learning WHEN to push and when NOT to push is the key. Teaching your fingers what to do and when to do it requires concentration, and practice.

Step One

Begin by grasping the needle between the first finger and thumb of the top hand, palm down, point down, with the eye of the needle firmly anchored in the dimples on the top of the thimble.

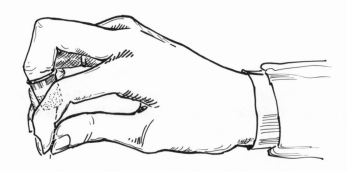

Needle held between first finger and thumb, point down,
with needle eye balanced in thimble top.

SET the point of the needle on the top of the quilt and remove the first finger and thumb from the sides of the needle. EXERT ONLY ENOUGH PRESSURE TO KEEP THE NEEDLE BALANCED ON TOP OF THE QUILT IN A STRAIGHT, VERTICAL POSITION. Rest the thumb on the surface of the quilt.

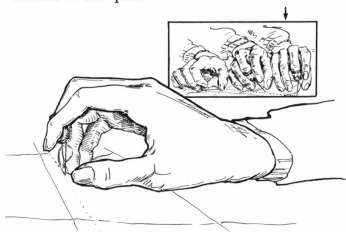

The thimble alone holds the needle vertical.

Step Two

Reach under the quilt with your bottom hand and rest the tip of your middle finger under the place you expect the needle to exit once it is pushed through the quilt.

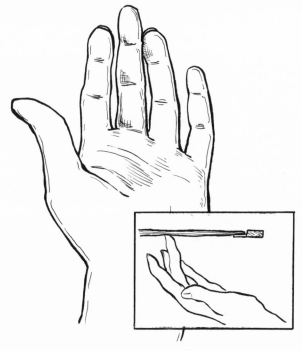

Bottom hand in position waiting to feel needle.

With a light touch, use your thimble to gently push the needle through the quilt. Remember to keep the needle in a vertical position.

As you begin to push, brush the middle finger on the bottom hand slowly towards you. The movement of the bottom finger in this manner heightens the feeling in the tip of the finger. This brushing movement should be very slight. You need only slide the point of the needle over two or three ridges of your fingertip to be sure the needle has exited the back. (You should be able to feel the needle passing over the ridges in the top hand, too.)

Pushing the needle at this point requires very little force. In fact, you may find that by simply positioning the needle on the quilt top, the tip of the needle has moved through all three layers. If it has, don't panic. Until you learn a lighter touch, simply pull it back up from the top so that only the tip can be felt underneath. Do not push it back up to the top of the quilt with the middle finger of the bottom hand. That hurts!

Remember, as soon as the needle is felt with the bottom finger, STOP PUSHING!

The amount of needle that has passed through the back of the quilt equals the length of the stitch that will appear on the back of the quilt once the thread is pulled through.

Step Three

Now that you have felt the needle with your bottom hand, it is time to change directions and begin to bring the needle back out through the top of the quilt. WITHOUT EXERTING ANY MORE DOWNWARD PRESSURE, OTHER THAN THAT NEEDED TO BALANCE AND STABILIZE THE EYE OF THE NEEDLE IN ONE OF THE

INDENTATIONS IN YOUR THIMBLE, move the top of the needle in a downward arc towards the surface of the quilt.

The thimble moves the needle in a downward arc.

Just after you have begun this downward arc, use the middle finger on the bottom hand to push up from the back of the quilt. Ideally the brushing action of the bottom finger should coincide with the very beginning of the arcing motion. After the point of the needle has passed the third fingertip ridge or so, and the needle has gone about one third of the way down the arc, it is safe for the bottom finger to push up. It will have cleared the point and won't get pricked.

Just after the bottom finger has begun to push, use the thumb on the top hand to push the quilt DOWN. Position the side of the thumb just after and slightly below (towards your wrist) where you anticipate the point of the needle to exit on the top of the quilt.

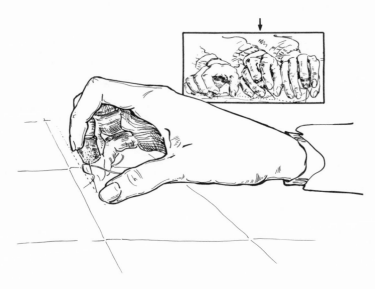

Pushing up from the bottom with the middle finger, pushing down from the top with the thumb.

Continue the arcing motion with upward pressure from the bottom finger and downward pressure from the thumb, until the needle is in a HORIZONTAL position, parallel to the surface of the quilt.

If you have done this correctly, you should notice a small hill or ripple in the surface of the quilt.

For smaller hills (and smaller stitches) the
position of the needle in relation to the quilt can
be slightly exaggerated so that the eye of the
needle dips below the flat plane of the quilt.

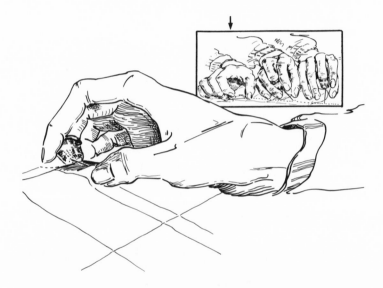

A small ripple or hill can be seen on the surface of the quilt.

Don't be afraid to push HARD. The more you
push with the middle finger underneath and the
thumb on top, the smaller the hill. THE
SMALLER THE HILL, THE SMALLER THE
STITCH!

Step Four

Now, you may push the needle through the
hill, remembering to keep the needle parallel to
the surface of the quilt as you push.

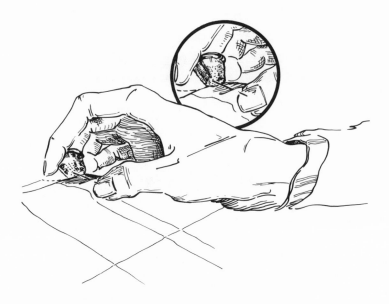

Push the needle through the hill.

If you have positioned your thumb correctly, and applied even pressure, the needle will pass out of the far side of the hill and glide over your thumb, just missing the tip of your thumbnail. Push the needle as far as you can, pull it and the thread the rest of the way through, and pat yourself on the back. You have just completed one stitch!

Continue quilting by repeating steps one through four. Make sure that, when each new stitch is begun, attention is paid to the distance between where the thread exited the quilt and where you will insert the needle to make the beginning of the next stitch. Stitches should be even and straight.

Rocker Quilting

Rocker quilting is the fastest, most accurate way to quilt. It gets its name from the movement your hand and wrist make as they push the needle through the arc from the vertical to the horizontal position described above.

The difference between single stitching and rocker quilting is that in rocker quilting several stitches are taken on the same needle before it is pulled through the quilt. The number of stitches depends on the length of the stitches, the pliability of the quilt, and the strength of the quilter's fingers.

Be advised, however, that only about a quarter inch of fabric can be manipulated onto the needle at any one time. Needles just aren't strong enough for any more. For some quilters, this may be only two or three stitches; for others, it can be up to five or six stitches. Measure each needleful in length of fabric, not in number of stitches.

To rocker quilt, follow steps one through four, until you are instructed to push the needle all the way through the hill in step four. Everything is the same until that point.

When rocker quilting, you must stop the needle almost as soon as it exits the hill, because the amount of needle showing indicates the length of the stitch on the top of the quilt. Then, continue with step five.

Step Five

WITHOUT EXERTING ANY MORE HORIZONTAL PRESSURE THAN IS NEEDED TO KEEP THE EYE OF THE NEEDLE POSITIONED IN THE INDENTATIONS OF THE THIMBLE AND TO KEEP THE STITCH LENGTH CONSTANT, move the eye of the needle in an UPWARD arc until the needle is again vertical.

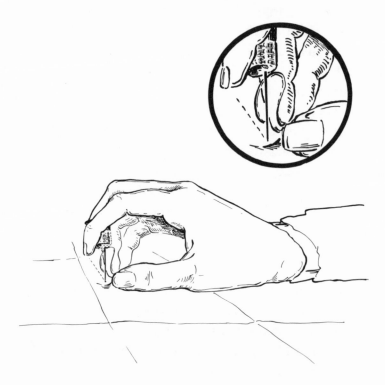

Begin the upward arc until the needle is vertical again.

It requires much more force to return the
needle to the vertical position in an upward arc,
than it did to make the first downward arc.

Once you have brought the needle to a
vertical position, the point is already in position
for the next stitch, ready for your downward
push and waiting finger underneath. Repeat
steps two, three and four until the number of
stitches, or their length, make it too difficult to
bend the quilt on and off your needle (about a
quarter inch of cloth). Then, push the needle as
far as you can through the series of hills and pull
the thread through.

When you begin with the next needleful, take
care to position the needle carefully for the first
stitch in the series, just as you would were you
quilting using the single stitch method. If you are
making very small stitches, you may have to pull
the thread from your last series of stitches out of
your way in order to see better.

Not surprisingly, these combinations of
downward and upward arcs, pushing with finger
and thumb, pushing with the thimble, and then
NOT pushing with the thimble but stabilizing the
needle instead, can be confusing. It seems as
though everything is going on at once! If this is
your first time and everything feels awkward,
don't worry. With a few hours of practice it will
become second nature and you won't even have
to think about it.

To set the progression of events firmly in your mind, read each step over again. Then read the next section which is a recap of the last several pages.

One More Time

1.   Hold the needle (first finger & thumb) with the eye anchored in one of the thimble's dimples.

2.   Release thumb and first finger.

3.   Push down as you prepare to feel for the point with the bottom finger.

4.   Brush needle point over fingertip to check penetration, begin downward arc. (Thimble is stabilizing, NOT pushing.)

5.   About a third of the way through the arc, finish the brushing stroke and begin pushing up from the bottom.

6.   Start pushing down with the thumb.

7.   Bring the needle to a horizontal position to form the hill.

8.   Push the needle through the hill. (The amount of needle showing equals the stitch length.)

9.   Bring the needle back up to a vertical position. (Thimble is stabilizing, NOT pushing.)

10.   Begin the next stitch by pushing the needle down as you feel for the point of the needle.

11.   Repeat until it is too difficult to make the arcs. Pull needle and thread through, and repeat from #1.

Helpful Hints

If you find it difficult to hold the needle with your first finger and thumb, and anchor the eye of the needle in the dimple of your thimble at the same time; try an alternate grip using the fourth finger and thumb.

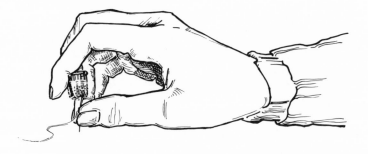

Alternate finger position using fourth finger and thumb.

The only disadvantage to this grip is that you must reposition your fingers after the thread is pulled and before the next stitch is taken, unless you pull with your fourth finger and thumb.

Until you become accustomed to this technique, you may find yourself pushing the needle too far into the quilt to make your stitches. Should the middle finger on your bottom hand become sore, give it a rest and try using your first finger instead.

Once you understand what is to be done, mastery is a matter of coordination. Expect that your stitches will get worse before they get better, especially if this method is radically different from what you are used to.

Avoid counting stitches until your hands and fingers are sure of what they are doing and their movements become almost second nature. Then concentrate on placement of the needle to get even stitches. Once they are even, work to increase your strength so that you can push hard and create the small hills which make for smaller stitches. Then work on the rhythm and pace to increase speed.

Watch each stitch as it is formed on the needle. Think about what you are trying to do each step of the way. It is legal to take out stitches that don't measure up, but ONLY AFTER YOU'VE GIVEN YOURSELF A CHANCE TO BECOME FAMILIAR WITH THE TECHNIQUE. Let the learning process be fun. Allow yourself to grow by accepting your skill at its present level, knowing that with practice you will surely improve.

CHAPTER VII

CORRECTING COMMON PROBLEMS

The Eye Of The Needle Slips Off My Thimble

Make sure the thimble you are working with has nice, deep indentations. If it doesn't, find a new one. If it does, check the angle at which it meets the needle. If it is at too sharp an angle, even the best thimble won't grab. Try moving your thimble so that the needle is perpendicular to the top of the thimble.

My Stitches Are So Big I Can't Make The Arcs

This is very common for people who have never tried this kind of quilting before. If you've already tried changing to a thin batting, short needle, good thimble, and all the other variables are in your favor, stick to the single stitch method for a while.

When you notice your stitches are getting a little smaller, try just two stitches per needle. Work up from there.

Also, make sure that you are using your thumb to push down from the top. Without pressure from the thumb, the hill will be too fat and the stitches too long.

The Top Looks Great, But I'm Not Catching Enough Of The Back

Chances are you are sticking the needle in at an angle. Check each time you place it on the quilt to make sure that it is straight up and down. Have someone else watch you to be sure. Sometimes you think it's straight when it really isn't.

Some Stitches Are Long, Some Are Short

As you sew, make sure your thumb is positioned correctly. It should not obstruct your view of the needle. You should NEVER use your thumb to feel for the point of the needle exiting the quilt top. If you do, you won't be able to tell precisely how long the stitch is going to be.

My Stitches Are Uneven! I Get Three Or Four Nice Short Ones, And Then A Big One! More Small Ones, And Then Another "Toe-Hooker!"

Large single stitches among otherwise even stitches is a symptom of poor needle placement with the beginning of each series of stitches. It usually happens when the thread from the last series is obstructing your view.

Use the pinky finger of your top hand to catch the thread and tug it backwards or to the side so that you can see where the needle should go.

Why Is The First Stitch So Hard To Make?

Bad news. The first stitch is ALWAYS the most difficult to make. That's the advantage of rocker quilting over single stitching. You only have to make ONE hard stitch per needle and the rest are easy. Single stitchers never get to make the easy ones.

CHAPTER VIII

BEGINNING AND ENDING

How To Begin

To begin a line of quilting, cut a length of quilting thread about 14 to 18 inches long, thread it through the needle, and put a knot at one end.

If possible, always anchor your knot in a seam allowance a very short distance away from where your first stitch will be.

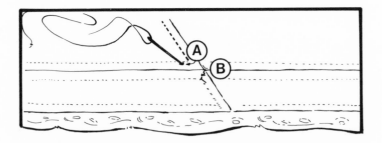

Enter quilt top through point A, pass THROUGH seam allowance, and exit at point B. Pop knot.

Pull the thread so that only the knot remains on top, and gently pop it through by stroking the knot in the opposite direction with your thumbnail. Take your fingernail and "scratch" the surface of the quilt in several directions so that the threads which separated to allow the knot to pass through will return to normal.

If, after several tries, the knot does not pop through, it may be too big. Cut it off and try again.

If you are quilting far away from seamlines you must anchor the knot in or under another existing or future line of stitching. In this case insert the needle a short distance away from where you will make your first stitch and weave it in and out of the batting as much as possible before it exits the quilt top. Be careful not to catch the back. All knots must be buried within the quilt and not show on top or bottom.

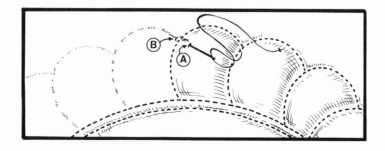

Insert needle at point A, pass needle through line of stitching and exit at point B. Pop knot.

If you prefer, you can just start quilting and leave a tail six to eight inches long instead of a knot. After you have finished the line of stitching, and ended using one of the methods presented in the next section, come back to where you started and rethread your needle with the tail. Simply "end" the beginning, too.

How To End

Many end by burying a knot in the nearest
seam allowance. After your last stitch is taken,
but before the needle exits the quilt top, move
your needle through the batting and up through
a seam allowance. Make a knot at the surface of
the quilt. Then go back through the same hole
that your thread is coming out of, and travel a
short distance away through the batting and
come out on the top of the quilt. Pop the knot,
and clip the thread.

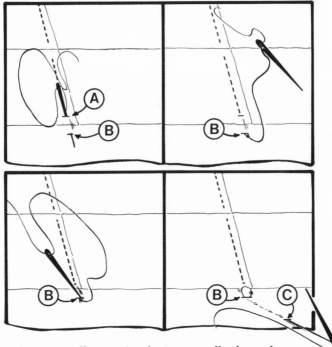

Insert needle at point A, pass needle through seam
allowance and exit at point B. Knot, insert needle at point
B, exit at point C and clip.

If there is no seam allowance to bury the
knot in, the next best thing is to plant it in a line
of future or existing stitches.

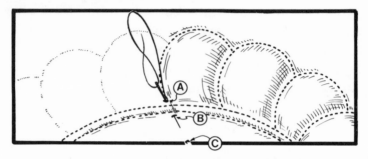

Insert needle at point A, pass needle through line of
stitching and exit at point B. Knot, insert needle at point B,
exit at point C and clip.

If there are no seams, or future or existing
lines of stitching in which to anchor the knot, try
the half backstitch method. It is better than
backstitching (which is NOT an acceptable
method of ending threads because it distorts the
quilted surface) but is more difficult.

When you are one stitch away from ending
and about to make the last stitch, insert the
needle AT A SLIGHT ANGLE. (A)

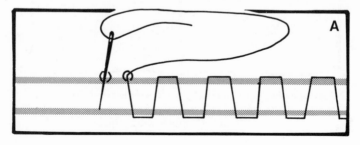

Push until it is felt coming through the back
of the quilt and begin your downward arc. (B)

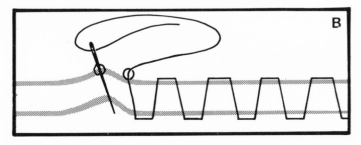

Since you are taking a backstitch, you will be
arcing in the opposite direction. Instead of arcing
the eye of the needle down toward the last
completed stitch, you will be arcing away from it.

The needle should exit the top of the quilt
through the same exact hole that the last thread
has exited, making a complete circle. (C)

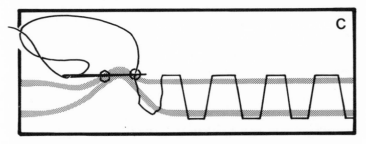

As you can imagine, this is twice as difficult
to do as making a regular stitch. Before pulling
the needle through, you must do two things.
First, look on the back of the quilt to make sure
that the needle showing through the back (which
equals the stitch length on the back) is even and
NOT touching the stitch next to it. It will be
slightly smaller than the rest.

Second, slide the point of the needle back just slightly, releasing the quilt top. (D)

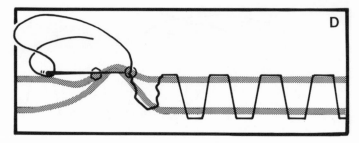

Then bring the needle forward so that it travels under the quilt top to the end of the previous stitch. (E)

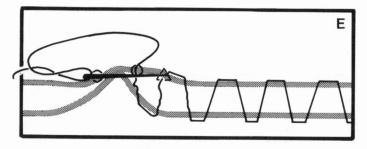

Bring it out and knot the thread at the surface of the quilt. Pass the needle under that stitch and through the top and pop the knot. (F)

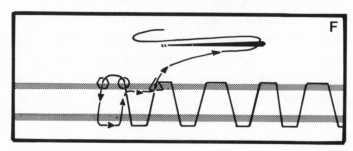

For those who aren't crazy about knots there is yet another method with which to end AND begin, shared by Phyllis Klein of Warwick, NY.

Take your last stitch so that it passes only through the top of the quilt and the batting, creating a "fake" stitch, and aim for an area above the line of stitching. Push the point of the needle out, then pull the needle by the point until the eye has cleared the line of stitching, but is still in the quilt.

Then, push the needle backwards, by the point, guiding the eye of the needle between the "fake" stitch you took and the one preceding it, just under the quilt top. Take care not to catch any batting with your needle. The needle should only go through the batting while making that first "fake" stitch.

Carefully push the eye of the needle through the quilt top. (Rubbing your finger over the eye of the needle will help to pop it through without damaging the quilt top.) Pull the needle by the eye until the point has cleared the line of stitching, but has not been pulled out of the quilt.

Guide the point of the needle between the next two stitches and push it out of the top. Pull the needle by the point until the eye has cleared the line of stitching, and guide the eye between the next two stitches. Continue weaving the thread between the stitches until the tension on the thread as you pull it satisfies you that the thread will hold.

Pull the thread, and clip. To relax any distortion caused by the weaving, stroke the woven stitches with your fingertip several times. This will be especially helpful if you pulled the thread too tight and your last stitch was swallowed by the quilt.

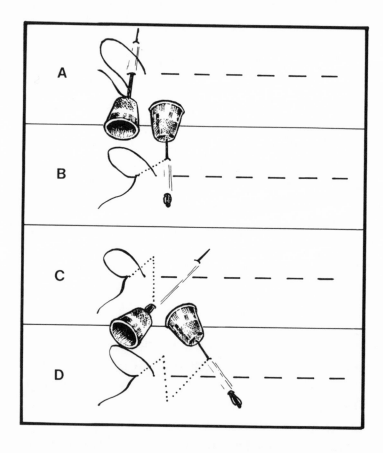

Weave the thread between stitches using the point and eye of the needle.

If you'd like to use this technique to begin and end, but are worried about "skipped" stitches on the back when starting and stopping in a continuous line of stitching, do what Amy Bunce of Wauconda, IL does. Instead of taking the "fake" stitch to end, insert your needle in the same hole that the thread is coming out of. Slide it under the top, just as before and begin weaving. Then, when you begin the next length of thread, insert your needle one stitch past where you want to begin and leave a tail. Come back and end the tail using the "fake" stitch method. The two will just meet without missing or skipping stitches.

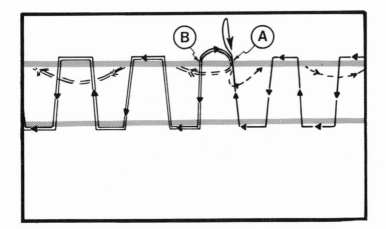

Two lines of stitching overlap.

EPILOGUE

The variables presented in this book can all work in your favor to improve your quilting stitch. Cotton fabric, thin batting, short sturdy needles, good thimbles, a "quilter friendly" environment, and a thorough understanding of how quilting stitches are made, can all contribute to small, even stitches. Individually or in combination, these variables can make the quilting process easier. It is now up to you to manipulate them to suit **your** needs.

APPENDIX A

NAMES AND ADDRESSES OF MAJOR BATTING MANUFACTURERS

Air-Lite Synthetics
342 Irwin Street
Pontiac, MI 48341

Crafter's Cabin
American Fiber Industries
5770 Peachtree Street
City of Commerce, CA 90040

Fairfield Processing Corporation
88 Rose Hill Avenue
P.O. Box 1130
Danbury, CT 06813

Heartfelt Wool Batting
RFD 340
Vineyard Haven
Martha's Vineyard, MA 02568

Hobbs Bonded Fibers
Crafts Projects Division
P.O. BOX 3000
Mexia, TX 76667

Jo-Ann Fabrics
Fabri-Centers of America
23550 Commerce Park Road
Cleveland, OH 44122

Maple Springs Farm
1828 Highway PB
Verona, WI 53593

Morning Glory
Taylor Bedding Mfg. Co.
P.O. Box 979
Taylor, TX 76574

Mountain Mist
Stearns Technical Textile Co.
100 Williams Street
Cincinnati, OH 45215

Putnam Soft Shapes
P.O. Box 310
Walworth, WI 53184

Superfluff
United National
3729 St. Louis
Chicago, IL 60632

Warm Products, Inc.
1232 120th NE #112
Kirkland, WA 98033

APPENDIX B

HOW TO FIND GRAINLINE

The simplest way to find the grainline in a piece of fabric is to look for the selvage edge, the tightly woven edge of the goods that prevents the cloth from raveling.

If it has been cut off, hold the fabric up to the light so the weave of the fabric can be seen. Align the fabric so that the lines are running vertically and horizontally and pull first in one direction, and then in the other. The straight of the goods (straight grain) will not give as much as the cross grain. The bias (diagonally) will stretch the most.

If you can't tell by pulling, try a method shown to me by a student in New Jersey. Snap the fabric! A sharp tug with the grain will produce a high-pitched "pop." A sharp tug on the cross grain will produce a lower-pitched "thud."

APPENDIX C

HOW TO GET USED TO A THIMBLE

Method #1: Get a good quality thimble and put it on right now. Don't read another word until it's sitting on your finger. Got it on? Good. Now don't take it off.

Wear it all day long. Wear it while you eat, sleep, and watch TV. Wear it when you grocery shop, drive the car, or take a walk. (You MAY take it off when you bathe, wear rubber gloves, or play the piano.)

Try to keep it on your finger until you don't notice it any more, and until it feels like a natural extension of your finger.

(Paint the inside of the thimble with a thin coat of nail polish so that you won't get rust stains on your finger; that REALLY looks funny.)

Method #2: Every time you sit down to sew, put the thimble on. No matter what. Force yourself to use it for AT LEAST THE FIRST TEN MINUTES. If it still drives you crazy after ten minutes, take it off for half an hour. Then try it again. Work to increase the time you are able to wear the thimble until gradually you will be wearing it all the time.

APPENDIX D

ILLUSTRATIONS FOR
LEFT-HANDED QUILTERS

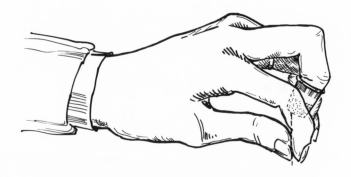

Needle held between first finger and thumb, point down,
with needle eye balanced in thimble top.

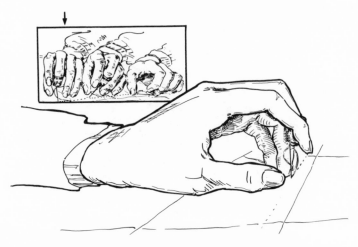

The thimble alone holds the needle vertical.

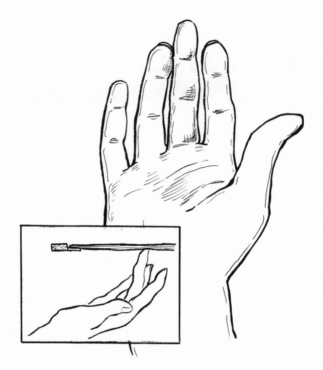

Bottom hand in position waiting to feel the needle.

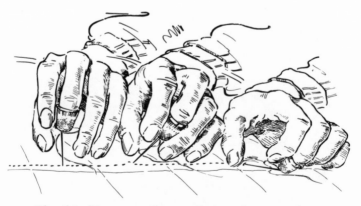

The thimble moves the needle in a downward arc.

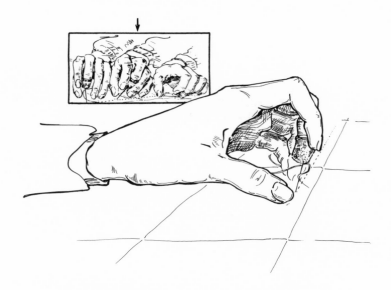

Pushing up from the bottom with the middle finger,
pushing down from the top with the thumb.

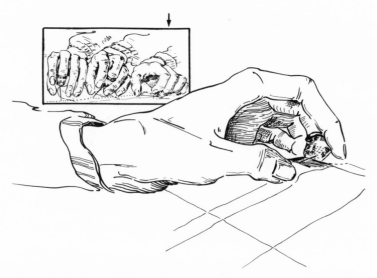

A small ripple or hill can be seen on the surface of the quilt.

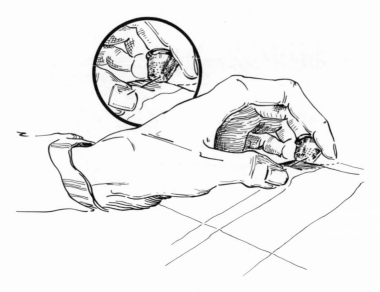

Push the needle through the hill.

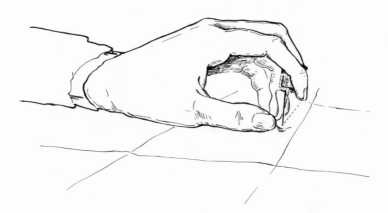

Begin the upward arc until the needle is vertical again.

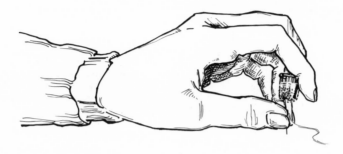

Alternate finger position using fourth finger and thumb.

Ending with a half backstitch.

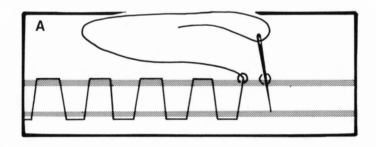

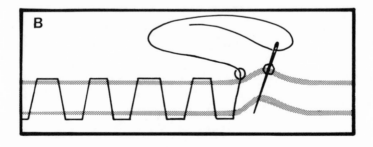

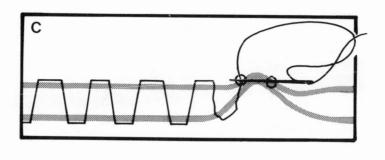

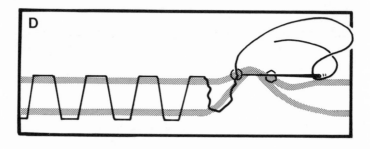

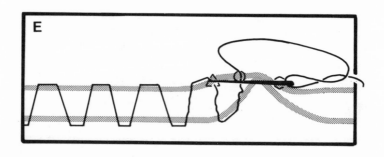

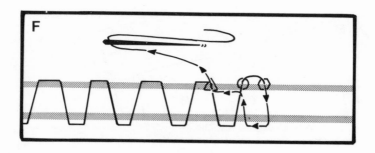

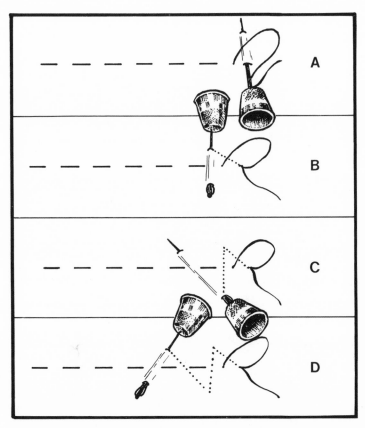

Weave the thread between stitches using the point and eye of the needle.

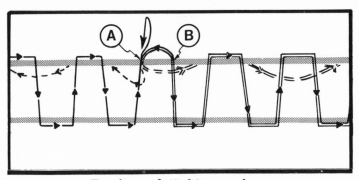

Two lines of stitching overlap.

For a free catalog of books by Ami Simms contact:
Mallery Press
4206 Sheraton Drive
Flint, Michigan 48532-3557 USA
Telephone: 1-800-A-STITCH or (810) 733-8743